Salt Moon

CRAB ORCHARD SERIES IN POETRY
FIRST BOOK AWARD

salt moon

POEMS BY
NOEL CROOK

Crab Orchard Review &
Southern Illinois University Press
Carbondale

18 17 16 15   5 4 3 2

The Crab Orchard Series in Poetry is a joint publishing venture of
Southern Illinois University Press and *Crab Orchard Review*. This
series has been made possible by the generous support of the Office
of the President of Southern Illinois University and the Office of the
Vice Chancellor for Academic Affairs and Provost at Southern Illinois
University Carbondale.

Editor of the Crab Orchard Series in Poetry: Jon Tribble
Judge for the 2014 First Book Award: Amy Fleury

Cover illustration: Original watercolor painting by Janet Biehl;
copyright © Janet Biehl; all rights reserved

Library of Congress Cataloging-in-Publication Data
Crook, Noel, 1963–
[Poems. Selections]
Salt moon / Noel Crook.
    p. cm. — (Crab Orchard Series in Poetry)
    ISBN 978-0-8093-3387-5 (pbk.)
    ISBN 0-8093-3387-2 (paperback)
    ISBN 978-0-8093-3388-2 (ebook)
I. Title.
PS3603.R6647A6 2015
811'.6—dc23   2014034608

For Will, Charles, Mary, and Richard,
and for my mother, who read to me

Contents

Acknowledgments   ix

DARK COUNTRY
Big Sky   3
Owl   5
The Slaves   7
Crows   9
Storm   11
Dark Country   12
The Twins   14
House   15

EVENING NEWS
Turner's Suns   21
On the Road to Agra   22
War Photo   24
Evening News   25
Skull   26
The Mistake   27
"Mercy"   28
The Secret Lives of Animals   29
Dog Heart   31
Demeter in the Pediatric Ward   32
Piano Teacher   33
Lice   34

NOTES FROM A SALT FLAT PRISONER
Melancholia   37
Orion's Belt   38
Notes from a Salt Flat Prisoner   39

Coyotes   40

Prey   41

Trap   43

Helen   44

At the Party for Her Husband   46

Bob & Wheel   47

On the Whitney Exhibition *Picasso and American Art*   48

Field-of-Flowers   49

     COMANCHE TRACE

Smith Canyon   53

The Sunday Swim, Comanche Trace   54

First Kill   55

Spotlighting   56

Matilda Lockhart, Age 13, Abducted by Comanches   58

The Horse Graveyard   59

Reading Ovid at Buzzard Rocks   61

Song   63

Acknowledgments

Grateful acknowledgment is due to the editors of the following publications, in which some of these poems first appeared, sometimes in different form:

The Atlanta Review: "Smith Canyon"
Birmingham Poetry Review: "Field-of-Flowers"
Crazyhorse: "Coyotes"
Great River Review: "Owl"
JAMA: The Journal of the American Medical Association: "Piano Teacher" and "Storm"
Main Street Rag: "Matilda Lockhart, Age 13, Abducted by Comanches"
The Normal School: "Lice" and "Skull"
One: "Big Sky"
Poetry East: "The Sunday Swim, Comanche Trace"
Potomac Review: "Reading Ovid at Buzzard Rocks"
Raleigh Review: "House," "Orion's Belt," and "Prey"
River Styx: "The Horse Graveyard" and "On the Road to Agra"
Shenandoah: "Turner's Suns" (as "J. M. W. Turner's Suns")
Smartish Pace: "Notes from a Salt Flat Prisoner"
Southeast Review: "Crows"
Tar River Poetry: "The Slaves" (as "Keeping the Bones") and "The Twins"
Wake County Physician: "'Mercy'" (as "Job")
Walter: "Dog Heart"
War, Literature and the Arts: "War Photo"

"Notes from a Salt Flat Prisoner" was printed again in *Best New Poets 2014*.

"Smith Canyon" appeared again in *Perfect Dragonfly: a Commonplace Book of Poems Celebrating a Decade & a Half of Printing and Publishing at Red Dragonfly Press* (Red Dragonfly Press, 2011), and in the anthology *What Matters* (Jacar Press, 2013).

"The Twins" was printed again in *Tar River Poetry, 30th Anniversary Issue*.

Several of the poems in this collection were included in the chapbook *Canyon* (Red Dragonfly Press, 2010).

Many thanks to Amy Fleury for choosing this book and to Jon Tribble and everyone at *Crab Orchard Review* and Southern Illinois University Press for their keen and patient editing of it. Deepest gratitude to John Balaban—poet, teacher, mentor, and friend extraordinaire—for his unflagging humor and guidance throughout the writing. Thanks also to Betty Adcock, whose poems taught me before I had the good fortune to know her, and to Claudia Emerson, Antony Harrison, Dorianne Laux, Peter Makuck, Tim McBride, and Joseph Millar for their generosity, kindness, and invaluable advice. Thanks to my teachers, especially Edwin Wilson, Lee Potter, and John Morillo, and to my cohorts in the North Carolina State University MFA program and the Wayward Ladies Poetry Circle, Eloise Gilster, Elizabeth Jackson, Kelly Michels, Nora Shepard, and Shannon Ward. And with abiding appreciation to my family, Eileen and Phyllis Vance, Bill Crook, and, mostly, my mother, Eleanor, and my sister, Elizabeth Crook, for their love and tireless encouragement along the road.

DARK COUNTRY

Big Sky

Little sky in these Carolina woods,
more greens than you can number,
above us crooked rafters of washed-out

blue. Here ten kinds of bird all hollering
at once, ten songs of secret nest and sifted
light. Here we are hemmed in by tendrils,

socked in, loblolly so high and thick
even the pasture's a cracked sarcophagus
where you have to look quick to locate the moon.

I want the western sky
of my girlhood, purple as lupines
and longing. Unligatured wind

that will hollow your bones
like the kiss of a boy at sixteen
who flattened me over the hot hood

of his Ram truck. Give me sun-stunted
scrub oaks rooted in rock and shaped like
bad hearts; the summer a mountain lion

ambushed an appaloosa colt by the barn
and two bottle-fed backyard deer, their bones
dragged to the dump to be picked clean

and sun-whitened. Give me found flint
arrowheads the color of lost rivers,
the barbed-wire fact that Comanche girls

liked burning the captured fawn slowly
to death before breakfast; scorched
earth, nights rampant with stars,

the Pleiades fleeing, an orange skiff of moon going
down fast into black swells of hills. Sunrise
the colors of cataclysm, the singular

solace of the canyon wrens, their strafed
ululations, and, in a cartwheel of azure,
the lone buzzard wheeling and waiting.

Owl

All day he stays hidden, his hole deep
in the grizzled oak that leans
and reaches past our bedroom window.

We find his leavings in the pansy bed:
dry orbs of bone and fur laced
with tiny xylophones of vertebra,

little femurs, sharp-chinned skulls.
Some nights I make him out, obscure
as a thumb-smudge on his porch

of bald white branch, a small dark dome
against the moon. We sleep
beneath him—beneath a shell

of shingle and plaster in a nest
of down from other birds, and surely
our sounds (the rustle of bedclothes,

the sighing of dogs) reach his owl-ears,
mix with the sweet scrabble of mice
in the woodpile. He speaks to the night

in round vowels that fur my dreams,
but if I could I would call him
to me some dark midnight, tell him

how once I heard the cry of something small
from the woods behind the barn—
a low pain-whistle that spiked my blood

—how that night from the hole of my sleep
I searched for it, briars tearing my nightgown,
the landscape topsy-turvy with my running.

And he would tell how he knows death as swoop
and smack of beak, the crush of small bones,
the kick of the whole mouse in the craw.

The Slaves

That first spring in the old farmhouse
we call ours, I found them, their stones
strewn in the wooded corner of the mares'
pasture, sloping into barbed wire, blackberry
thicket, toward the creek below—a few
uncertain mounds nudged by roots
of loblollies, shifted by erosion.

They are nothing like those ordered rows
of Faithful Wives, Beloved Sons
in the Zion churchyard down the road,
but the earth remembers
with its smattering of March narcissus.
Who in secrecy or careless grief
dug the bulbs, dirt-smelling
and heavy as promises, from the neat ring
around the backyard oak?

Summers, our children use the pond washstone
for a diving board, their toes grip
its curved surface smoothed by calloused hands
and sheets and petticoats. We show visitors
the old quarters:
                    "Seventeen slept here,"
we say. "The bunks must have been three high."

I should tend them, these jumbled dead,
straighten their stones, smooth their cracked turf,
put up a small fence—the kind found on country drives
past old homeplaces that confine death
to a square—but there is no figuring where

their heads lie or even where the graves end.
Perhaps string wind chimes from pine branches,
but those dull tones might be unbearable.

No, let them have their confusion
of peepers in the spring, in the fall
the bay of hunting dogs, the knock
of horse and deer hooves
over their dark rooms. Let them have
the rib's slow deliverance through red clay
into cattails—at the creek's bank
the blooming of teeth
in the grass. *Let lie, let lie,*
the veery sings, but the earth turns
and turns and will not keep.

Crows

What is it the crows know this first real day of fall
when the sky's gone vacuous and the air thins?
They bark on the lawn in their raucous code,

plumage blue-black smoke of a city
smoldering. Already they have performed
their daily harassment of the owl,

old hunchback in his snag in the backyard oak,
have communicated the exact coordinates
of the buff-colored cat and patrolled

the bedraggled roses where our best dogs
are buried. They wing in from Indian mounds
down in the woods, the back pasture

where slaves' headstones list in the fescue.
Last week I found a black widow fisted
and gleaming in the sandbox—scarlet hourglass

against black carapace—and this morning
over the bubbling of oatmeal, the low drone
of war on the television set, I felt it again:

that pang that comes with the changing
leaves, frail unease as the world tilts again
into winter—some forgotten drumming

in the marrow that should have me filling
the woodpile and rasping the axe.
The crows call in threes:

Watch, watch, watch. Shadows of wings,
they say, and gather the seeds.
Count the children again.

Storm

How quickly the heart hunkers down for the worst,
like the day the whole East Coast braces
for a Category 4 and you're just digging candle stubs
from the kitchen junk drawer when the school nurse
calls to say your daughter's gone partially blind
in math class, her right arm dead, and by the time
you drive her to the pediatric ER, one stump-numb
hand pressed like a sick child to her breast,

you have already practically rented a wheelchair,
seen her face pale against hospital sheets,
whirr of the respirator, wiped drool from her cheek,
the words *no* and *please* wheeling like seabirds
against shredded clouds of your brain—
old tuneless song of the lost sailor's mother,
unscathed and *unscathed* and *unscathed.*

And in the exam room, under noxious fluorescents,
you number her bones while the nurses enter
and leave and you think of lifeboats,
the huge clock above her blind as a moon,
till the doctor arrives to tell you
how the CAT scan was clear, MRI clean, something
unfathomable: potassium levels, her not eating lunch.

Then you breathe what feels like the first clean breath
of the blue-lipped rescued, just breathe and breathe
the entire way home, don't even think of the storm
still lolling over the Atlantic, leisurely dragging
its malignant heart toward shore, the candles left strewn
on the kitchen floor, how later you'll watch her
sleep in their frail circle of light.

Dark Country

Night presses its Rorschach shadows
against kitchen windows I haven't bothered
to curtain yet. Who'd prowl these rutted

back roads anyway? Who'd even find us
out here? But the dog disagrees. All day
he stares me down and begs me to attend,

nudging the empty food bowl, dropping
onerous offerings of scalped tennis balls,
a mysterious stiff sock dug up in the woods,

the tiny, perfect wren discovered feet curled
under the azaleas. Now he growls
at his own reflection in the storm door

and circles our girl reading by the fire,
levels his anvil head on my knee,
and whimpers when I finish folding sheets.

At this hour the barn cats are at their ebullient
murders again. We'll find gifts of jeweled
entrails on porch steps come sunrise: *This*

is how it's done, they say. Last winter
the 11-year-old twins across Tabbs creek—
eyes blue as March mornings, shorn hair

the color of orioles' wings—stockpiled bullets
for weeks, then cut the phone cords and waited
for the ring of their father's footsteps

on the stairs. The dog cocks his ears
for what we can't hear: rustle of small atrocities
in the moon-silvered fescue, sudden

bright chuff of a doe startled by footfalls
in pine needles where gloved hands
might push back branches

and the spark of a lit porch would catch
the eye of any wayward soul. The girl shifts
and sighs on the sofa, pink bra strap slipping

to her elbow, and the dog whines,
locks his eyes on mine
and will not sit.

The Twins

Their teachers said they hadn't noticed
anything amiss, but I wasn't a bit
surprised when the sheriff called that morning
to tell us what they'd done,
their mama shot and left for dead, their father
with his head blown off.

A neighbor found them rocking on the porch,
one of them crying that the rabbit hutch
was open and his bunny had got out.
We found out later that they'd used
their birthday gifts—two Rugers—
and their father's own shotgun as a backup.

I happened on them once, hiding in a bunker
they'd dug out down by our creek, gibbering
in that twin-speak that would light up your spine.
"If you see those boys in the woods, you hightail it,"
I told my own babies, "and if they follow you,
you say your mama's on to them."

Some months before it happened, I phoned their father
when I caught them fooling with our yearling colts.
He showed up in his fatigues. "That bay," I said,
"will break their necks." When he got them home,
we heard the yelling all the way across the creek.
Good, I'd thought, that'll be the end of it.

House

Swaybacked, molting, mildew-blackened
    between fallow tobacco fields,
        its sprung shutters sagging

like flagged wings, the house foundered
    under the oaks when we came,
        fresh from the city and just married.

An exercise in history, we learned that slaves
    had built the place—at the courthouse ferreted out
        Captain Archibald Capehart's deeds

for fourteen unnamed field hands who'd loaded
    oak beams numbered at the mill
        and hauled them by wagon

down twenty miles of mud road,
    dug a cellar out of red clay.
        Now it sits, squat, white as an egg

at the end of the dirt drive, smug
    in the coat of paint we gave it
        last spring, and in the time it's taken

to find the right green
    for the master bedroom and bury
        three good dogs out back, we've learned

the crooked landscapes of its unplumb
    walls, their blunt odor of horsehair wadding
        on afternoons when damp slicks

the corrugated roof and mold grows
    on our shoes in the mudroom;
        on winter mornings the frail

constellations of spackle-dust sifted
    silent as strychnine from the cracked hall
        ceiling. The walls here are swollen

with stories—blank-faced, serene, they keep
    secrets of whole families held
        restless and musty in the plaster:

the caught breaths of children playing hide
    and seek, slow crumbling
        of marriages, little treacheries

of brothers, smell of another brought in
    unnoticed on a husband's hands.
        In my daughter's room the cry

of the mother whose boy died
    in her arms, skull smashed
        when his Roadster missed the curve:

our own stories sidled up next
    to those of Captain Capehart, laid out
        and bathed on the dining-room table,

all the mirrors hung with sheets.
    Hot nights, when sleep swings
        out of reach, the windows thrown open,

I hear them confabulating behind the plaster
    —dry, querulous whispers threaded
        with the trilling of the crickets—

and half-dream how someday
    the house will fall, victim of a faulty wire
        or deserted in some end-of-world

disaster, the wind lifting its tin lid for rain,
    thin laths loosening, all our stories
        sliding into mud—how maybe it will stand

for a while like this, a dark skeleton
    against the pines, marker only for those
        who moved silent over pitched joists,

matching and joining the beams,
    the ring of their hammers rising
        into blue, immaculate sky.

EVENING NEWS

Turner's Suns

His pupils must have been tiny as pinheads
when he painted that brightness—stood small
and wild-haired before gigantic seascapes
evaporating in their terrible light.
From his own darkness he gave his brush

to red, the molten pupil of his God's-eye;
thrust yellow to the top of canvases
where it bloomed
and fell, a mushroom cloud of saffron
vapor under which not one thing is spared—

ships sinking, sailors stricken, even
monsters half-hidden in the waves roiling
at being seen, whole coastal towns exposed,
irradiated, so that the smallest shadow
would be something to crawl into.

To stand beneath one is to know a little
of what it is to raise your face to the thing
that could take you in an instant, not
to ask for its mercy but to open your palms
and show it your throat.

On the Road to Agra

Monsoon was overdue and I remember
how that morning in Old Delhi the sky turned
pewter and drops the size of rupees pocked
the asphalt, how from the backseat
of the hotel car it seemed the entire city
was glad. Even the beggars in Chandri
Chowk—the pretty mother proffering
her pinwheel of broken fingers, soft cheek
of a new baby at her breast; the boy
who a day before had followed, tapping

at our windows—lifted up their faces to the rain
and smiled. On the outskirts of town
along the brown Yamuna, elephants
hauled lumber in their great freckled
trunks, bony children straddling their withers,
and the gorgeous brahmas, sleek
and entitled, napped in busy streets,
their dark flanks patterning with rain.

And later, I remember how the gypsies rose
like fumes from the flat stretch of highway ahead,
a thin mist of drizzle causing us to mistake their bear
for a burly man till the car slowed and stopped,
and there was the lank rope strung through its nose,
the frothed V of lower lip, one eye just
pink flesh of empty socket and, when the rope
jerked taut, its vague, sad dance,

our quick scrabbling for loose change —
and I do not remember how the window opened
and they reached for our money,
only how black their eyes were
without the glass between us, the chill spit
of the rain in our faces, how the coins slid
from our hands, and in Agra the river already swelling
past its banks, the Taj rising pale as a tear,
how we paid them to look away.

War Photo

On the tiled floor of a hospital,
the girl is turned and bathed, arms raised
as if to Allah, only a small wad of cloth
pulled between her legs to cover her nakedness:
waist not yet narrowed, tiny nipples dark
punctuation marks of unwritten sentences,
the perfect wishbone of mandible exposed
that ten years down the road a lover might have kissed.

In the morning she will be wrapped
in white cloth, but now her body glistens
with the wet of sponges, careful as cats' tongues.
Above her, the black-robed mother stares
into the camera's lens, her own eyes
dark as holes, saying to thousands,
millions of eyes, every eye on earth,
Look. This is what it is.

Evening News

Though she received a single bullet wrapped
in her death notice, the Iraqi grandmother, Umluma,
did not believe that they would really kill
an old woman (*Yes, Dear*, she said when the shooter
called her name. *Can I help you?*).

       And now it seems reform
of Romanian orphanages has not gone as hoped:
heavy-breasted, diapered teens sway in cribs;
a spittle-lipped boy strains at his ropes.

       In Colorado,
a girl tells how she closed her eyes but heard
unzipping of her classmates skirts, the ripping
of their clothes, and cannot forgive herself for living.

Lord, Lord, up and down the street, through darkened
windows, televisions flicker like blue, rheumy eyes.
Satellites are spidering cold orbits, their dishes
gray faces raised, waiting. Across the tangled
ganglia of airwaves through subterranean
networks of cables travels the news,
the stories fleeting, relentless as prayers.

Skull

Why did the owner of the black van
parked outside the Snack & Pack have a skull
hanging from his rearview mirror?
My children did not notice,
but it eyed them through dark sockets,
sighed though hollows of its slack jaw.

Tonight, from my bed, I watch
the hallway leading to their rooms —
one who throws the covers off, his arms
and legs flung wide like a sea star;
one with a dog at her feet and three dolls
tucked in neatly, their bristled heads
on the pillow beside her; one who
murmurs in his sleep for pancakes —

and all night I consider my options, my own
black capacities: the baseball bat
nestled in the toy chest, its satisfying
weight and heft; a claw hammer gleaming
in the toolbox; in the kitchen, the cool handle
of the butcher knife that fits the palm like an answer.

The Mistake

So you've had a "lapse in judgment," a close call,
and suddenly I am the grim-faced prison matron,

while you—who have perfected
the fifteen-year-old's eye roll—grow sullen.

Pet, boy of my heart, with your easy charm,
your straight A's, they are out there,

your various fates, prowling the periphery
of your good life, waiting to be realized,

to set off whispers of strangers and nights shot
with regret: a bullet in the chamber

and the safety off; the baby in the tub
and the telephone rings; your eyes

taken from the road for just a moment
when everything is changed and you are left

remembering that only a moment before,
this was your worst mistake,

the worst thing you ever did. Listen,
I should take your lovely head, your face

with its first shadow of down, its thickening
mandible, pound it on some unyielding surface

of the unforgiving world, and then rock you
while it still can be made better.

"Mercy"

Sure Job was impressive, a poster child
for God, stuck in his land of Uz
but never quibbling, his great house burned,
livestock driven from his fields,
the throats of his servants slit, and worse:
his beloveds smote by a single, sudden wind.
But surely, when the boils appeared,
bone-rooted, bursting their way to ooze
through acquiescent flesh, and he sat down
in ashes to wish himself unborn, to scrape his sores
with a potsherd, the maggots falling about him
in small ecstasies, just once, behind
the cracked sphincter of his lips he tongued
the forbidden, fruitless word.

The Secret Lives of Animals

One chicken I have loved, bought with my own nickel
at the Feed and Grain when I was nine, taken from my arms
when he outgrew the wire cage beside my bed, stood tiptoe,
and opened the red flower of his throat
to the sun.

Three children I have raised to their season of breast-bud
and first shaves, and in the hothouse darkness of their rooms
their desires tendril into places
I cannot nurture.

Seven dogs have I loved, including the rescue with a taste
for his own shit, not least the childhood spaniel mix
who made quick work of my best hamster. And now this
small white terrier, bred to please, who shimmies with joy
when she greets me mornings, whose best friend is the gray
cat, half prince of sofa-shadow, half Jeffrey Dahmer,
that—if the dog were smaller and the timing right—
might lick her heart.

And who am I to unlove the terrier for her descents
into the cat's basement workshop—uncollared dark
from which she returns, tail wagging, bearing a crenulated,
meat-tipped wing or garnet-throated chipmunk head? Once,
at my oldest's age, I brought home to my own mother
a necklace of hickeys, crimson as suns, each mouth-shaped
mark a talisman of want's slow burn, secreted in my mind
the look of the boy with freckles and red hair,
his lip pulled back to ugly snarl when I undid
the buttons on my dress.

At night, the young dog shimmers like a moth across the grass,
and, though invisible in shadow, I know the cat flits
in tandem, lets her flat-back him in the mulch, purrs ecstatic

when she mock-mauls his upturned gullet—wild pantomime
of hungers I can and cannot fathom, while *Here sweetling,*
I call her. *Here wildling. Come to mama.*

Dog Heart

He lies still, breath clouding the slate tiles
between his paws. Only the occasional twitch of an ear
mars his perfect vigil. He has grown old
following the girl, his only lamb; has watched her

since a diaper rustled at her thighs.
Now she is gone all day
and he waits for her here by the door.
He has contemplated the demise of the mailman,

who moves too close when he hands her packages;
has dreamed the warm brine of the bus driver's blood.
Do not misjudge this old dog--
beneath dull fur and steepled bones of his ribs

runs the keen rush of valve to ventricle,
the old thrill of a bared tooth.

Demeter in the Pediatric Ward

When they'd come before dawn,
wielding thermometers and rattling
their scales, she'd be standing by the door,

hair wild, no lipstick, to tell them
they'd better not be waking me up
for nothing. Down cold fluorescent hallways

we'd come rolling after treatments, her tripping
on the stretcher wheels, and she'd send the nurses
packing, smooth my pillow, sometimes slip in bed

with me, our little silver-sided barque.
From the world outside the sun slipped through
venetian blinds and she measured sorrow

in small cups of ginger-ale we'd sip
through frail bent straws. How could I not
press my face into her belly, trace the blue,

raised veins in her hands? She'd turned to
mist in the hall while I lay with the devil
in the knifed light of the treatment room.

Piano Teacher

The disease has taken a blitzkrieg turn:
synapses at the bottom of his cortex
seize as neurons thicken to dark sludge.

What seemed a stiff knee is now a jester's dip
and lurch, his elbows flap permissionless.
Wild rhythms mortify him, his eyes widen

with the wrath of them, the swoop and rock.
Before, when a student butchered Beethoven,
he'd cut in—*Listen!* he'd say, *Listen to this!*

—and launch into something brilliant
by Rachmaninoff, change the subject quickly with
a Joplin rag. Now his hands muddle

even the thunder of his dear Mahler.
Forgive me, he says, to the child who sits
lumpish beside him, to Mahler,

to the black notes that still fly across the page
of his mind, their music perfect and elusive as birds.

Lice

We have seen the enemy—she on the tip
of her pencil when she scratched her head,
I, in the school nurse's office. Now, in a sunlit
corner of the kitchen, we spread

the poison through her hair. I won't tell her
of the egg sacs, fat with young, stuck fast
to the strands, the gray nits swarming
in the down behind her ears where flesh is softest.

Like an executioner I lay the dead out
side by side on the counter tiles. She eyes my
little morgue. She is having second thoughts:
what about their mommies? *Hush*, I say.

At her temples the fine veins pattern in the sun.
She will be host to nothing, to no one.

NOTES FROM A
SALT FLAT PRISONER

Melancholia

Who is this knocking at my door?
I should not but will let him in

since he is sadmouthed and solemn
and pretends to know me best.

Love, he says, come here to me,
put out your lip so I can bite it.

Let me see those tears, my love.
Forget the children sleeping down the hall,

the toothbrush in its cabinet, dishes
congealing in the sink. Ah, Love,

he says, come here to me. You see?
He does not even know my name.

Orion's Belt

All those years he loved
the smallness of her hands—

how the fist fit neatly in his palm,
his fingers circling both her wrists

at once. In bed he admired
the winnowing of rib to waist,

the rise of hip; contemplated
her flank, her ankles, her feet.

Of course he worshiped
the obvious: breasts, belly,

the darkness there between her legs.
But even when she showed him

he did not see she kept Orion's Belt
in a splay of freckles on her thigh.

Notes from a Salt Flat Prisoner

Bonaire

On this island, love, there is nothing but black
and white—the sea's flat back that keeps us,
bleak shards of coral honed sharp as knives
by tireless wavelets. And the salt—vast,
blinding pans for us to rake. It galls
our wrists and shins like manacles.

Nothing grows here but these crystals. Even
the dark seaweed swirling in the inlets
rises on spindly legs as if to swim
away. Small black lizards whisper
names of home against the dry rocks
and we boil them for it. We are sick

of fish. All day the sun's blanched eye
seeks us, and not one rock
big enough to hide under. I am changed
by this place—like Lot's wife
I look back, reconfigure
the purple shadows in the struts of your

ribs, your tongue in my mouth like pure fire.
Here there is no holy water or sin.
Each night we bathe ourselves in brine,
lie under a black collar of sky, the spume
of white salt stars, the salt white moon,
the sting of crystals blooming on our skin.

Coyotes

What is it the coyotes are after,
casting their loose nets of need
through the night sky? There are some

who'd laugh at them—the torn fur and low,
ratty tails, stomachs shrunk to their spines,
most days existing on the odd frog,

a sluggish locust—but any rancher
will tell you they leave their mark:
a stray hen gone, the old barn cat

missing. Last summer, a neighbor's
retriever took off into the bald hills
with a shadowy pack. We have called

and called. They are a godless crowd,
but from them we could learn a thing or two
about devotion: how one should own

the indelicacies of desire,
the dragged belly, the rough gutturals
of real begging. All night

they jibber on scrawny haunches,
supplicants offering their jugulars
to a white bone moon that, if they could,

they might fell in an instant,
wallow in the cold, downed light.

Prey

It was the eviscerated porcupine,
its sacrificial posture over the downed
poplar limb, buck teeth tipped back

in what seemed like surrender, innards missing
from a belly split clean as a hickory nut. Then later
that month, the doe downed in the backyard,

neck snapped but otherwise left whole,
the three weanling calves just plain gone
from the neighbor's pasture that made us think not

of recent rumors of mountain lion kills
in Medina, but of Uncle Winfred, long eaten
by colon cancer, his campfire tales

of the *hrumphrumph* that once prowled
these bluffs, hungry for hearts, especially those
of girls who ventured out at night.

And though he did not speak of height
or conformation, in our dreams we conjured
our own—mine lean, yarn brown, and loping.

Loose-hocked it paced through gorse shadow
when the pickup idled and we'd draw straws
to see who had to shimmy from the truck's bed

to unlatch the gate, even the youngest unexempt
from that long trek down the limestone aisle
of road, taillights crimsoning our thighs.

At dinner the conversation turns
to the neighbor's foreman, who last week
cut the throat of a young goat and slung it

from a cedar sapling, crouched all night
with a Colt .45 by a bucket of blood, but nothing.
Still, after the dishes are done, some of us

slip out alone to walk the chalk-pale loop
past the barn, under a caul of stars,
our faces silvered by a reaper's moon.

To know again how our hearts are meat,
what it would be to be husbanded
by something marrow hungry, imagine again

what bloom-pupiled beast skulks through darkness,
lifts a muzzle to the perfume of our flesh.
To have a name for it.

Trap

And who hasn't been there? Think
checking shirts for lipstick marks, rummaging
through briefcase pockets for a note,

a number, anything. Think Othello's
green-eyed monster, jilted Sappho's slipped
mind, *a slender fire racing* under her skin,

or Vulcan, twisted over his forge,
the thought *trap* thrusting like rough sex
through his brain, his humped shadow

thrown against the wall, spittle from thin lips
hissing on the flames while he hammered
out each link for the mesh he'd snare

her in, never stopping to think
how it would end: her shoulders gleaming
like knives in the sunlight, bright hair blinding

against the net; how he'd have to fumble
with blunt fingers at his own knots to set her
loose and she'd just fix her jeweled girdle

and walk away, still beautiful and not his.

Helen

No one ever mentions it,

    least of all Homer, whose concern

was mostly with the gods'

    maneuvering of her lover,

and then his breach of palace etiquette,

    and all that bloody honor.

No one tells how her dress fell

    onto the cold stone, how when

she curved her arms above her head

    the smell of her own sweat

stung her awake;

    how she stood naked for him,

knew the length of her white throat

    bent back, the slope of her hips

when he parted her thighs

    with his knee and took her;

why she let herself be taken

    in darkness, wrapped like contraband,

left her brothers and her grown son

    to be secreted in the ship's hull

that reeked of fish and piss

    and rang with footsteps of his men

as it slammed the waves toward Troy.

At the Party for Her Husband

In the receiving line,
the man with alarming breath
tells her she is charming.
She is trapped by heels
just high enough to hinder flight;
her suit is black wool crêpe,
nipped slightly at the waist,
and the wife of the man more important
than her husband takes her hand
to remind her that behind each powerful man
is a strong woman.

She wonders what the guests might say
if she unzipped her skirt,
let it fall around her ankles,
lifted the jacket from her shoulders,
let it drop behind her to the floor,
then proceeded to the skin,
peeling it back in one great layer,
the veins, like a blue nest of spiderwebs,
the fascia, the muscles, all removed,
until she stood there by her husband,
ribs shining, each neat round bone
in her spine chittering and clacking.
She says, *I don't believe we've met.*

Bob & Wheel

The man at the bus stop watched
the girl pass. Of course he knew
she had not dressed for him.
The jeans that hugged her hips
like a boyfriend's hands,
her aubergine mouth,
narrow heels that ticked
the sidewalk as she neared
were not for him.

For him there was her sudden sensing
of his cigarette, the registering of his
yellow smile, her gaze glued
to the sidewalk, swift check
of the buttons on her blouse.
      For him that
      quickened step,
      the faltering look back,
      arm pressed against her breast
      were aphrodisiac.

On the *Whitney Exhibition* Picasso and American Art

Of course there was the moxie of it,
angles appearing like answers
everyone else had missed; later, dismissing
the ubiquitous knockout nude, flattening,
hatch-planing into the dull curve of flesh.

And though he never stepped a small black shoe
into America, New York teemed with copycats,
the avant-garde all trying their hands
at slice-and-dice. Critics blushed to tell how vulvae,
sharp as sharks' teeth, centered canvases

and pudenda dangled like great dumb mouths.
Now, in the gallery, crowds murmur and mill,
hands clasped behind their backs,
while Lichtenstein's *Girl with Beachball II*
(breasts drooping from shoulders like stricken limbs)

cries a single cartoon tear. Jasper Johns' *Untitled*,
a sorrowful purple, weeps red from one good eye.
Those of us who have them stand cross-armed
before tits detached, refashioned as epaulets;
cross-ankled in front of labia pasted onto cheeks.

Later we will stand in the bright fall light
of Madison Avenue to check parts
reduced to measurable units, ponder
how once a genius flourished the blade
of his brush and made dismemberment the rage.

Field-of-Flowers

If you have traveled five thousand miles
to make a decision—to Istanbul, say—
do not expect elucidation
from the Call to Prayer or the color of a new
ocean. The slow, sad cries of the muezzins

ricocheting through the domed city are not
for you and the bay will sparkle like a blue,
unblinking eye, the word *Bosphorus*
ungainly as borrowed jewelry.

In the caged heat of the Hagia Sophia,
the mosaic faces of the martyrs will be anything
but resolute, and, in the Architectural Museum,
under formaldehyde light, the odalisques on loan
from the Musée d'Orsay will sprawl blank-eyed

in their flat, elaborate worlds, though one will wear
nothing but a skirt like the silk hijab that whispered
past your fingers in the bazaar, shimmering
Aegean blue, spangled with silvered moons.

On the sun-struck steps of Taksim Square
where touts hawk their stained-glass lanterns
made in China, a man might be offering
young rabbits to hold, but he is really selling

small scrolled fortunes. And while you can touch
the soft fur, the man will be watching,
his eyes the color of gunpowder, the fortunes
at his feet like a basket of bullets.

Do not look for respite
in the shop with its sign for "Cooled Air,"
where the rugman will unfurl ground
after jeweled ground at your feet, pour black tea
into hourglass-shaped cups and say,
Each rug tells a story,
                                        or look for direction
in the weft of the ancient Field-of-Flowers
from a village where women are allowed only
undyed fleece of white and black or rare brown sheep,

even if you are the one to notice in the far, top corner,
not a stain, but three tiny, illicit tulips tendriled
—*a wish for love*, says the vendor—
even if something in those bright knots

splits the day in half, something in the turn
of petal, where crimson carves into dull wool,
like the place where wish snaps into regret,
in the colors she used, must have chosen
in secret, thrilling as stolen fruit.

Do not ask if she bought an azure silk skirt
that brought a lover to his knees, if she laid him down
on an ottoman mattress, under the racket of locusts,
under grapes and fiery skeins of wool curing.

Sip the obligatory tea, watch the vendor
roll the rug up tight to cram it back into
the rack, the question of price
still hanging in the air.

COMANCHE TRACE

Smith Canyon

That summer when loss took me by the throat
I came home to the parched Texas hills, in late
August a bleached-bone color, the grasses sallowed,
white caliche roads shrouded in thin dust.

I drove to the canyon—a great scar, beautiful
in the way of a scar, in the story it tells—
where a child can trace the stone swirl of a mollusk
big as her father's foot, and the cliffs are whales

that swim endlessly, tattoos of humped and eyeless
trilobites embellishing their flanks;
where along the steeper sides the untouched ledges
tease with their pale stippling.

The mind canvasses them, lies along them,
crouches in crevices cool with the chalky smell
of millennia. Comanches camped here,
chipping arrowheads at the water's edge.

Under the persistent wheeling of the buzzards,
I walked the rocky shore, sank deep in the dark water
until green and fingering reeds brushed my hair, glad
that once the cliffs had whispered

with the scuttling of a million blind crustaceans.
I was their sister, the warm sun whitening
my bones, the curve of my spine
another decoration on the limestone floor.

The Sunday Swim, Comanche Trace

The canyon ledge was steep and stark,
the pool below a patch of dark.

The canyon wrens careened our names
and from the narrow overhangs

the lupines leaned and clung, like us,
to any purchase they could muster.

We grappled down the frowning rock
then bolted for the swimming dock,

slowed to strip down to our skins,
the bullfrogs plopped to beat us in.

Other children, dark and bare,
had bathed and played and squatted there

and left us shining arrowheads
along the rocky water's edge.

The velvet slime squeezed through our toes,
the water greened our feet and rose

around our hips and pulled us in,
filled our arms and cupped our chins.

Its coolness seeped into an ear.
The minnows threaded through our hair.

We floated there along with clouds,
clouds our ceiling, clouds our ground.

First Kill

They threw the carcass from the truck
and you stood there, small and haloed
by red taillights, with mud and blood
of wild pig like war paint
on your face. *Look*, you said,
and swung the flashlight on the thing.

A dead eye glinted in the beam,
the vacant cavern of its gut
emitting mournful steam.
You'd cut the throat yourself,
curved your own knife through the belly,
pulled the entrails out.

I touched your little wrist
and traced the blue life pumping there.
I kissed your face, grown older
in a night, and kicked the dog
that would not leave the meat.

Spotlighting

> *When the lambs is lost in the mountain, he said. They is cry.*
> *Sometime come the mother. Sometime the wolf.*
>   —Cormac McCarthy, *Blood Meridian*

Who knew what was out there
those wind-whipped nights we clung
to the pickup's corrugated bed, a million

miles away from the comets' tails
of dashboard lights, smoke trails
of our father's cigar, crackling voices

from the AM station in Bandera.
Armed with flashlights we sailed
through thin night air—small Argonauts

crowded on chilly wheel hubs and dangling
the frail bait of our legs
over the tailgate's edge, passing

shadows that rose furred and shifty
behind the big, pale tears
of the prickly pear, the humped scrub oak

and shaggy-barked madrone. And though
our rumbling engine split the night,
the night folded deep and cobalt

back on us. Out past our dusty wake,
outside the rouge of taillights, the darkness
harbored anything. We did not

tease it with our feeble beams—instead
aimed hard into close twisted branches
that sparked with varmint eyes.

The white caliche roads lay down
in our headlights, uncertain
as the Milky Way in all that blackness.

Possum, we'd shout. *Coon*.

Matilda Lockhart, Age 13, Abducted by Comanches

No doubt she'd have made it
back across Plum Creek to the field
where her father plowed, the rifle strapped
to the mule's back, had she not stopped

to drag her little brother, searching for pecans
by the water's edge. Two years
they whittled away at her and she endured
like a specter in their camps, each night waiting

for dawn, when they'd char her face and feet again
with breakfast embers—and she would not let herself
remember her mother blowing on a skinned knee,
her father whipping the teacher who'd rapped her knuckles.

A cousin found her half-starved, tied to a wagon wheel
on some muddy street in Bexar—something
about a birthmark on her cheek or the color
of her hair. But in the end it was the clean sheets,

the sound of her mother weeping,
her father's quick looks and silence that made her
touch the hollow where her nose had been
and shut her eyes for good.

The Horse Graveyard

for Jackie

Those summers before blood stickied
our thighs, chests bony as sparrows', we trekked
to the neighbor's pasture where we kept

our ponies, riding bareback till dusk,
straw-haired and feral under the wide sky—
our own 30 acres of Eden. We knew things then:

what it was to slice into green cool
of the pond down to the flat rock where we sat
cross-legged like war-chiefs; how speed

could swallow us, take us till it was all
there was, stealing our breaths, manes
stinging our cheeks. *Trust, trust,*

our ponies' feet sang in the tall grass.
But I should also tell how in the empty hours
we snuck to the burn-pit—kicked our horses

down the dusty road past "Keep Out"
signs until they would not budge,
tied them to branches of scrub oaks,

their nostrils flared, raw pink membranes
all dread, then rounded the corner on foot
to where dead horses lay blackened

on their sprawling pyres, the stench
of their unburned parts souring the clearing,
their hides like matted rugs. We picked our way

to the bleached bones of the long-dead, hunkered
to our job of prizing molars from their jaws
to trade at the bead seller's for turquoise rings

we'd wear to the movies on Friday nights,
our heels planted hard against the skulls
for the lurch of unsocketing.

I should tell how while we worked
the buzzards coughed and thumped
along the ground, their scorched meals

interrupted, then wheeled above us
as we trotted the shortcut through a sallow keloid
of cornfield toward the barn, our plunder

clacking in our pockets. Black wings
thrummed sluggish rhythms
we had not even thought of yet, whispered

the torpor of slow dances, slur
of too much beer, languor of hot backseats,
and the slow turns of betrayals—

how that next summer or the next
we left our ponies waiting in their field
while we went out to plumb the world.

Reading Ovid at Buzzard Rocks

April, and I've come back to this blunt horizon
butting up against a bell jar of blue
and a sun that can bake the meat off anything,

even loss. Where if you hold out your arms
at the bluff's edge and breathe deeply enough,
the sky will agree

to swallow you whole. But it's turkey mating season
again, the lovelorn, dusty hens congregating
over on Horse Hill, scooting willy-nilly in

and out of sage and prickly pear, addled
by their need, and the water
I cool my feet in is the same

pale cataract that once spilled
past me as a girl when I sunbathed
on the dam, dreaming of the boy I'd kissed

at summer camp, whose mouth drowned out
Led Zeppelin's "Stairway to Heaven,"
his breath on my neck, the way my heart let go

its dry tap-dance, floundered like a downed
bird, the weight of his hands like ballast on my hips—
and the hens scatter and drift haphazard as ash,

waiting for kettle-drum calls of the gobblers
roosting solitary and oily in the cottonwoods,
their bristled beards swinging

like scalp belts. After this long coyote winter,
all of us still wanting to be stitched
into the old cloth of the world's desire,

still wading these shallow waters, traipsing
these same parched hills, waiting for the sudden
shadow blocking out the sun, the beating

of wings, something, anything, to pin us down
under all this blue sky.

Song

Last night on Horse Hill they were howling
for the moon to come down, their voices
zigzagging the canyon like heat lightning

till our house turned small on the cliff's lip
and the moon blanched to a small white scar.
From our beds we imagine them out there,

yammering for what they can't have—jaws
unhinged, furred necks bent back,
the ragged belly-deep vowels of yearning.

Once, as a girl, when my own need undid me,
the boy I loved indifferent as the moon,
I tried it—crept in my nightgown

to where the chalk bluffs give way
to blackness, crouched, mouth open
to an O. But my arms shone blue and hairless

under a bleached gibbous, and from the scrub oaks
the raccoons' eyes glittered. Even
the stars watched from their dark bowl

and the song stuck like a bone in my throat.

Other Books in the Crab Orchard Series in Poetry

Muse
Susan Aizenberg

Millennial Teeth
Dan Albergotti

Lizzie Borden in Love:
    Poems in Women's Voices
Julianna Baggott

This Country of Mothers
Julianna Baggott

The Black Ocean
Brian Barker

The Sphere of Birds
Ciaran Berry

White Summer
Joelle Biele

Rookery
Traci Brimhall

In Search of the Great Dead
Richard Cecil

Twenty First Century Blues
Richard Cecil

Circle
Victoria Chang

Consolation Miracle
Chad Davidson

From the Fire Hills
Chad Davidson

The Last Predicta
Chad Davidson

Furious Lullaby
Oliver de la Paz

Names above Houses
Oliver de la Paz

The Star-Spangled Banner
Denise Duhamel

Smith Blue
Camille T. Dungy

Seam
Tarfia Faizullah

Beautiful Trouble
Amy Fleury

Sympathetic Magic
Amy Fleury

Soluble Fish
Mary Jo Firth Gillett

Pelican Tracks
Elton Glaser

Winter Amnesties
Elton Glaser

Strange Land
Todd Hearon

Always Danger
David Hernandez

Heavenly Bodies
Cynthia Huntington

Zion
TJ Jarrett

Red Clay Suite
Honorée Fanonne Jeffers

Fabulae
Joy Katz

Cinema Muto
Jesse Lee Kercheval

Train to Agra
Vandana Khanna

If No Moon
Moira Linehan

Incarnate Grace
Moira Linehan

For Dust Thou Art
Timothy Liu

Strange Valentine
A. Loudermilk

Dark Alphabet
Jennifer Maier

Lacemakers
Claire McQuerry

Tongue Lyre
Tyler Mills

Oblivio Gate
Sean Nevin

Holding Everything Down
William Notter

American Flamingo
Greg Pape

Crossroads and Unholy Water
Marilene Phipps

Birthmark
Jon Pineda

Threshold
Jennifer Richter

*On the Cusp of a Dangerous
  Year*
Lee Ann Roripaugh

Year of the Snake
Lee Ann Roripaugh

Misery Prefigured
J. Allyn Rosser

In the Absence of Clocks
Jacob Shores-Arguello

Glaciology
Jeffrey Skinner

Roam
Susan B. A. Somers-Willett

The Laughter of Adam and Eve
Jason Sommer

Huang Po and the Dimensions
    of Love
Wally Swist

Persephone in America
Alison Townsend

Becoming Ebony
Patricia Jabbeh Wesley

Abide
Jake Adam York

A Murmuration of Starlings
Jake Adam York

Persons Unknown
Jake Adam York